The Essential Bu

CW00970162

Honda
SOHC FOURS

CB350, CB400F, CB500, CB550, CB550F, CB550K,
CB650, CB750, CB750A, CB750F, CB750K
– 1969-84

Your marque expert:
Peter Henshaw

VELOCE PUBLISHING
THE PUBLISHER OF FINE AUTOMOTIVE BOOKS

Also from Veloce –

www.veloce.co.uk

First published in April 2010 by Veloce Publishing Limited, Veloce House, Parkway Farm Business Park, Middle Farm Way, Poundbury, Dorchester, Dorset, DT1 3AR, England. Fax 01305 250479/e-mail info@veloce.co.uk/web www.veloce.co.uk or www.velocebooks.com.

ISBN: 978-1-845842-84-0 UPC: 6-36847-04284-4

British Library Cataloguing in Publication Data – A catalogue record for this book is available from the British Library. Typesetting, design and page make-up all by Veloce Publishing Ltd on Apple Mac.
Printed in India by Imprint Digital.

Introduction & thanks
– the purpose of this book

The single overhead cam Honda fours were milestone motorcycles. The original CB750 launched in 1969 made a huge impact, offering a previously unheard of specification   four cylinders, electric start, front disc brake, 120mph performance – at an affordable price. It turned motorcycling upside down, and was a huge hit. Honda went on to make over half a million of them.

The bike spawned a whole generation of big four-stroke fours from Kawasaki, Suzuki and Yamaha. But for Honda, the 750 was just the start. It was followed by the CB500, 350 and 400 fours, each one offering the same concept of a four-cylinder bike that coupled high-revving excitement with typical Honda refinement and reliability.

That was over 30 years ago, but even now these Honda fours can make good practical classic bikes. They are fast enough to be fun, while modern brake pads and tyres make them safe to use in today's traffic. Honda fours might lack the ultimate adrenalin of a wild two-stroke from the same era, but they are arguably more adaptable, able to go two-up touring with reasonable comfort, and (except for the 750) relatively cheap to run.

This book is a straightforward, practical guide to buying a Honda four secondhand. It doesn't list all the correct colour combinations for each year, or delve into the minutae of year-by-year changes – there are excellent books listed at the end of this one which do all of that. But hopefully it will help you avoid buying a lemon.

The nice thing about Honda fours is that, although they are all based around the same format, there's a huge range to choose from: the truly miniature CB350 (said to be Sochiro Honda's favourite model), the café racer CB400, the all-round middleweight CB500 and 550, the often overlooked CB650, and of course the one that started it all, the CB750. Any of them will deliver the authentic Honda four experience, but each in a slightly different way, so whatever your inclinations or budget, there should be something here to suit you.

Thanks are due to Annice Collet at the VMCC Library, to John Hoskison of On All Fours, and to Mark Manley. Also to Tim Parkinson, Reg McKenna and Paul Fairfax for the CB500/650 pictures.

Essential Buyer's Guide™ currency

At the time of publication a BG unit of currency "●" equals approximately £1.00/US$1.50/Euro 1.20. Please adjust to suit current exchange rates.

Contents

Tall and short riders
The CB750 suits six-footers, as it's a big, heavy bike. Shorter riders should go for one of the smaller fours, which still offer exciting performance in a manageable package.

Running costs
Modest for the 400/4, 500, 550 and 650, but the 750 will always cost more in consumables – you pay for the performance. Expect 50mpg from the small fours, but as little as 35mpg from the 750. In the UK, all pre-1973 bikes are exempt from road tax.

Maintenance
Needs to be kept on top of, but relatively straightforward. The frequent oil and filter changes are easy to do, and other routine jobs can be done without special tools.

Usability
Very good. All Honda fours are smooth and tractable on the road, with strong electrics and good reliability. Given regular maintenance, they can still be used as everyday bikes.

Even a non-standard four can make a fun classic bike.

Parts availability
Generally good, but patchy. Honda will still supply many parts, but some bodywork items are becoming hard to find. Many spares are available as patterns, though the quality isn't always up to Honda standards.

Parts costs
Quite reasonable. Honda service items are well priced, some (seats for example) are expensive, while pattern parts are invariably cheaper.

Insurance group
Depends on the bike (obviously the 750 is in a higher group than the 350!), but all Honda fours are eligible for limited mileage classic bike policies, which offer lower premiums. In the UK, Carole Nash and Footman James offer classic policies.

Investment potential
Limited. Rare bikes like the CB750 K0 and specials like the Seeleys and Dresdas will always command a high price, but the other fours are too numerous to represent an investment. That said, none of them will lose any value, and a 100% original example of any Honda four should fetch a good price.

Foibles
Correct maintenance (oil changes, camchain and brake caliper especially) is essential to keep the bikes running well.

Plus points
Relatively smooth, tractable engines with Honda reliability. The 400/4's excellent handling and 750's mile-eating capability. The Vintage Japanese Motorcycle Club is a good source of knowledge and camaraderie.

Minus points
Four-cylinder engines sound busy and buzzy compared to twins, which doesn't suit everyone. Brakes and lights aren't up to modern standards, and CB750 handling is fine for touring only.

Alternatives
Plenty for the 500/550/650/750, in equivalent four-cylinder Japanese bikes, but there's no direct equivalent to the CB350/4 and 400/4. Two-strokes from Suzuki, Yamaha and Kawasaki offer a very different riding experience.

Parts availability, especially for service items, is generally good. For some models, certain parts like mudguards, tanks and badges are now unobtainable new, but because of the number of bikes around there is usually a serviceable secondhand alternative. The small and middleweight fours should be quite cheap to run, giving 45-50mpg (even more with a gentle rider), and classic insurance policies are good value. The 750 will always cost more to run. Parts prices quoted below are from a Honda parts specialist, and comprise a mixture of Honda and non-Honda items for different models. Prices will vary – this is a selection.

Complete restoration (basest case to concours) – around ●x10,000
Air cleaner element – ●x9
Big-end bearing half shells (ea) – ●x5.5
Brake caliper complete – ●x149

Quality pattern parts are a good alternative.

Brake caliper piston – ●x27
Brake lever, front – ●x5
Brake master cylinder repair kit – ●x23
Brake pads set – ●x19.95
Brake shoes – ●x16
Battery – ●x26
Camchain – ●x36
Camchain tensioner – ●x21
CB points – ●x11.5
Clutch cable – ●x10
Clutch kit – ●x37
Clutch plate, metal – ●x4.95
Condensor – ●x4.5
Cylinder head gasket – ●x15
Engine service kit – ●x55
Exhaust (complete) – ●x399
Final drive chain – ●x29
Fork oil seal – ●x4.95
Fork stanchion – ●x69
Front mudguard – ●x89
Fuse box – ●x35
Gearbox mainshaft – ●x30
Handlebar switch – ●x45
Ignition coil assembly – ●x110
Inlet valve – ●x9.95
Oil filter – ●x4.1
Piston and rings (each) – ●x32
Primary chain – ●x55
Rear shocks (pair) – ●x125
Seat – ●x189
Seat cover – ●x19
Tank badge – ●x27
Taper-roller steering head kit – ●x27
Wheel rim (rear) – ●x33
Wiring harness – ●x125

Side reflectors are difficult to find, but service items are no problem.

Some side panels are still available.

3 Living with a Honda four

– will you get along together?

The Honda fours are quite easy to live with, and certainly not as maintenance-intensive as the average British twin. In the early 1970s they were thought of as complicated pieces of machinery, but by modern standards they are not. There are no electronics (apart from electronic ignition on the CB650), and nearly all parts can be dismantled and serviced.

In fact, the Hondas are relatively straightforward to look after, with no special tools or skills needed for the routine operations. Although regular servicing is vital, it's also quite simple: the oil filter is very easy to get at (though not to remove if the bolt's rounded off) and camchain tension is simply a case of loosening the locknut, allowing the tensioner to take up the slack, and retightening.

Valve clearances need to be checked every 5000 miles, and an eye kept on plugs and contact breaker points, plus the usual attention to tyres, chain and sprockets. But unless the bike needs repair, that's about it. The middle plugs are quite awkward to get at, especially on the 750 with its bigger, wider engine, and the front brake caliper needs some real TLC, with regular doses of WD-40 (well away from the pads) to keep the pivot moving freely – if it seizes, so will the pads.

There's an old adage to the effect that oil is cheaper than bearings, and it's as true now as it ever was. The most crucial aspect of maintenance for these bikes is regular oil changes. Most specialists recommend changing both oil and filter at least every 2000 miles (some say 1500), and it can't be stressed enough that this one action does more than any other to ensure a long, trouble-free engine life – gearbox and clutch too, as they all share the same oil supply. If you're not covering many miles each year, change the oil at the end of each riding season, so that the bike is put into hibernation with its bearings sitting in fresh oil. Given the short mileage intervals, it's not worth paying extra for synthetic oil – a 10/40 or 15/40 mineral oil is ideal, but don't use 20/50.

Given this sort of treatment, Honda fours can be very long-lived, with mileages of 50-60,000, even up to 100,000 miles, with little major work other than a rebore. Of course, the problem with any bike over 30 years old is that very few come with that sort of verifiable service history. You might be lucky, but the best to hope for is evidence of a

Could you get on with this bike?

more caring recent life, since the Hondas were marked out as classics.

So what are they like to ride? A lot of people are put off the idea of a classic bike because of the perceived hassle of extra maintenance, dodgy electrics and mechanical frailty, but that's not really the case with these Hondas. Apart from the frequent oil changes, maintenance isn't onerous, they have reliable 12-volt electrics, electric start and indicators; they are comfortable and will cruise

A shiny 750 will get you noticed!

at motorway speeds all day long without ill effects (assuming they're in good shape to start with).

Make no mistake, these bikes are from a different era, so they will seem a little crude and noisy compared to a 21st century water-cooled machine. Bear in mind that the youngest of them is over 25 years old, and the earliest CB750s have seen four decades. The braking isn't up to modern standards (though it's adequate, even on the 750), the lights aren't too hot, and you'll have to juggle with a manual choke on cold mornings – even contemporary road tests complained that Honda fours were picky about choke settings, and took a while to warm up.

Otherwise, all of these bikes have easily enough performance to keep up with modern traffic, and there's no reason why any of them shouldn't undertake a high mileage tour, or even be used as day-to-day transport – some of them still are, though most are now used as second or third bikes on sunny weekends.

One big advantage is that there's a whole range to choose from, with quite different characters and capabilites. Which model might work best for you is dealt with in more detail in Chapter 4, but the CB350 offers an enjoyable (if not fast) introduction to Honda fours in a small package. The 400/4 is something of a biking icon, especially in the UK. It is fast enough to be fun and has very good handling. A lot of people agree that the CB500, 550 and 650 are excellent all-rounders, more relaxed than the small fours but without the weight and bulk of the 750. That of course, remains the ultimate Honda four for many: a big heavy bike, but still impressively fast, very comfortable and able to go touring.

Whichever of these you decide on, there's a whole community out there to back you up. There isn't quite the guaranteed spares coverage that you'll find for, say, an old Triumph twin, but there are several specialists with a wealth of experience to offer. The Honda Owners Club and Vintage Japanese Motorcycle Club (especially the latter) are well worth joining, the VJMC being a good source of bikes, parts and know-how.

Buy the Honda four that suits you, look after it, and you should be rewarded with years of fun motorcycling – they make a great compromise between a British or Italian classic and a modern bike.

This chapter shows, in percentage terms, the value of individual models in good condition. There were many variations on the theme, and this chapter also looks at the strengths and weaknesses of each model, so you can decide which is best for you.

The Honda fours basically comprise three families: the CB350 and 400/4; the CB500, 550 and 650; and all on its own, the 750. Although there are significant differences between them in performance and character, all are based around the same format of an air-cooled four-cylinder single overhead camshaft engine, with a five- or six-speed gearbox, tubular steel frame and chain final drive. There's a lot of choice within the format, including mini-tourer (CB350), café racer (400/4), do-it-all bike (CB650) and superbike (CB750). Which one is best for you depends on your priorities and what you want out of the bike.

Range availability
CB350/4 1972-74
CB400/4 1975-77
CB500/4 1971-73
CB550K 1974-78
CB550F 1975-78
CB650 1979-82
CB650 Nighthawk 1980-82
CB750K 1969-78
CB750F 1975-78
CB750A 1976-78

CB350/400
The baby Honda fours were in fact the last ones to join the family, and at the time several

The 350/4 is the baby of the family.

journalists asked why Honda bothered. The company already offered the top-selling CB350 twin, and the CB350/4 turned out to be heavier, slower and more expensive. As a result, it wasn't a big seller, its appeal not helped by the fact that it was given quite sober styling, with an upright riding position and four-into-four exhaust system.

The engine was a miniaturised version of the CB500, with wet sump lubrication plus the plain bearing bottom end now familiar from the bigger bikes. With 34bhp at 9500rpm it could reach 98mph, but needed much stirring of the gear lever to make progress.

On the other hand, it does have a charm all of its own. One is rarity value, as far fewer 350s were sold than any other four, and the model was never officially imported to the UK. Another is character – accept the 350 as a smooth, mild-mannered mini-tourer, and it begins to reveal an attractive side to its character, being refined and easy to ride. There's also the fact that Sochiro Honda himself declared that the CB350/4 was his favourite of the roadgoing sohc fours, and there's quite a cachet attached to owning an example of the great man's best ride.

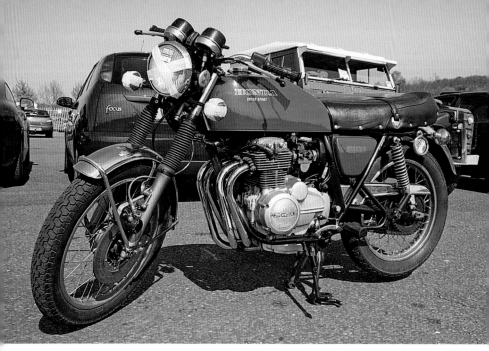

400/4 is a different – and sportier – prospect.

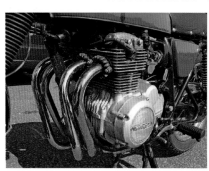

400cc four is a lively little motor.

'Super Sport' badge arrived with the 400/4.

Despite there being few around, the CB350/4 costs slightly less than an equivalent 400, and they do tend to collect a crowd. There's much to recommend seeking out a 350, if you can live with the performance and staid looks.

All this changed in 1975, when the 350 was replaced by the 400/4. Out went the touring stance, in came the newly fashionable café racer styling, with lower bars, rear-set footrests and plain solid colours. The centrepiece of the new bike was its four-into-one exhaust system, all four pipes curving seductively down to meet the single silencer. The makeover was so complete it was hard to accept that underneath much was the same as the 350; its frame and front end were still shared with the 350cc twin.

But there were significant mechanical changes, too. The motor was bored out to 408cc, giving 37bhp at 8500rpm, more midrange grunt, a top speed of 105mph and sharper acceleration. A six-speed gearbox added an overdrive ratio to the 350's five-speed box. The press loved it, hailing the little 400/4 as the best handling Honda yet, and it did handle, in an age when Japanese motorcycles tended to have engines that outran their chassis.

The 400/4 still has to be revved to get the best out of it, but owners will tell you that this is part of the fun. They will also tell you that few bikes (maybe even today) offer such accessible excitement, and the 400/4, complete with its

400/4 is much easier to find than the 350.

adrenalin pumping 10,000rpm red line, remains a very light and easy bike to ride. It will happily trickle along at low speeds, as quiet and courteous as the 350, even if it doesn't look it. The front disc/rear drum brakes are up to the performance as well.

There are plenty of 400/4s around in Europe and especially Britain, where it became something of a cult bike – Honda sold over 73,000 of them in Europe, though less than 10,000 in the USA and Canada. So there's plenty of choice in the secondhand market. There's no real advantage in seeking out a particular model, as Honda barely changed it in the four-year production run. The pillion footrests were moved from the swingarm to a frame mounting in 1976, and longer cylinder head studs were fitted from engine number 1084315 in an attempt to cure oil leaks. The F2 of 1978 was a purely cosmetic change, with new colours, pinstriping, and the fuel filler moved to one side. Some colours are more sought after than others (yellow is popular) but what really hits the value of a 400/4 is obviously non-standard fittings such as an aftermarket exhaust.

Strengths/weaknesses: Best choice for the shorter rider and novices. Lighter and easier to manage than the big fours. Engine needs revving for speed, but cheap to run, with good spares backup and great fun to ride.

CB350/4: 75%
CB400/4: 100%

CB500, 550, 650

After the runaway success of the CB750, Honda launched the CB500 in 1971 to try and repeat the trick in a smaller package. On paper, the 500 really was a 750 in miniature: four-cylinder sohc engine, electric start, front disc brake, tubular steel frame. In practice, it weighed 80lb less than the 750, had a lower seat and a wheelbase two inches shorter. Honda had tried hard to keep the 500's overall size down as well, so it was altogether more manageable, where the 750 could be something of a challenge for smaller riders.

The 499cc motor delivered 50bhp at 9000rpm, and road testers reported a top speed of around 105mph, with 45-50mpg. Handling was not quite as sharp as that of the little 400/4, and could be compromised by sticky forks and under-damped rear shocks, but it was good enough, and one specialist says that with modern tyres the middleweight fours are transformed.

These bikes were designed to appeal more to European tastes than the bulky 750, and the immediate recognition points are smaller trumpet-shaped silencers (four of them) and the engine mounted upright in the frame. Honda made few changes to the CB500 in its three-year run, so as with the 400, there's little advantage in seeking out a particular year.

In 1974 Honda announced the CB550, a reaction to Suzuki's GS550. Bored out to 544cc, it offered little more outright power than the 500, but more midrange, and though it was 30lb heavier, it was quicker on the road and could still average 50mpg. The following year it was joined by the 550F, a styling job that aped the 400/4 with swoopy four-into-one exhaust and a simpler paint job. 1977 saw the 550F2 with new paintwork, and a retro-style 550K with four pipes – there were no mechanical differences between them.

The 550 personifies these middleweight fours as the great all-rounders. Lighter and easier to hop onto than the big 750, they are less frenetic and more comfortable than the 400, especially two-up or when carrying a pile of luggage. Some owners seek out the CB500 as the 'purer' of the two, but the 550 is easier to find and tends to be lower priced, while its better mid-range power makes it more rideable.

The CB650 is something of a cinderella among Honda fours. It's often overlooked, because the company launched it alongside the more

CB500 is thought to be the 'purest' of the middleweight fours. (Reg McKenna)

500/550 models never sold as well as the 750, but are a good choice today.

650 lacks the classic styling of the older bikes, but could net you a bargain.

glamorous double overhead cam CB750 and 900 in 1978. The idea was to plug the gap between the CB550 and new 750, whilst countering Kawasaki's very popular Z650. It was soon overtaken by the 550 as well, which was replaced by a twin cam bike in 1982.

The 650's engine was a bored out version of the old 550, with redesigned top end and gearbox. There was a new frame, but many other parts came from Honda's existing bin, including the 750KZ's fuel tank, Comstar wheels and (for Europe) the bulbous rear light of the CX500. So the dowdy looking 650 was dismissed by many as a parts bin special with an ageing heart.

In practice, the 650 has much to recommend it. It had the CB750's brakes, but in a lighter chassis, so stopping power was good. The riding position was comfortable without being too upright and it also handled well, far better (thought some) than the heavy new twin cams. It was economical too. Electronic ignition was a worthwhile update, as was a semi-automatic camchain tensioner. The 650 really continued the tradition of the old 500/550, offering the four-cylinder experience in a lighter, more manageable package than the 750.

In 1980, the 650 was joined by the custom-styled Nighthawk, with teardrop fuel tank, pulled-back bars and forward-mounted footrests. Reviled at the time by many, this still makes a period piece, if you can find one. In fact, 650s in general are now rarer than 550s. They do suffer from top-end wear if oil changes are neglected, and don't have the classic styling of the other Honda fours, but there's much to recommend the 650 as a practical everyday bike.

Strengths/weaknesses: Good compromise between small 400 and big 750, with the 550 in particular making an affordable all-rounder. 650 lacks the charisma, but is a very nice bike to ride.

CB500: 122%
CB550: 101%
CB650: 119%

CB750

This was the bike that started it all, and for many the CB750 remains the definitive Honda four. It created a huge impact when it was unveiled at the Tokyo Motorcycle Show in 1968. Here was a motorcycle with truly exotic features and astounding performance, but at a price many people could afford. As one magazine put it, the big Honda offered the excitement of a superbike, the comfort of a Harley 74 and the touring ability of a BMW.

The bike that started it all, and still plenty to choose from.

Compared to a modern big bike, the 750 is heavy and not that fast, with wobbly handling, but it still has undeniable presence on the road. Slow is a relative term, and even the most stifled 750s could top 110mph, with 125mph possible on early bikes. It will easily cruise at 80mph all day, hauling two people and their luggage without a murmur, and return 40-45mpg.

If there is a downside, it's that the 750 is physically big and awkward to handle, and its sheer weight and power mean that it's quite heavy on consumables – chains last around 5000 miles. The single front disc (except on the final F2, with its twin front discs) has its work cut out too

Unlike the other fours, the 750 had a long production run, and there were changes over that time. The most sought after models are the rare K0s, with sandcast crankcases that have a rougher finish than the later diecast items. The K0s are no better to ride than the later bikes, but their rarity (Honda made only 7414 of them) makes them highly sought after today, and expensive. Another K0 recognition point is the small seat hump, which no other CB750 had.

Late model F2 with twin front discs and Comstar wheels.

Some spares for the K0 750 are unobtainable now, including side panels and badges, the airbox, seat, some switchgear and the chainguard. A more practical all round choice is one of the later K1s or K2s, which have far better spares backup, are easier to find and more affordable. Of all the 750s, the K1 was the best seller, followed by the K3 and 4. Apart from the K0, prices reflect condition rather than model. For many collectors, the four-into-four exhaust remains a key part of the 750's appeal, so an aftermarket four-into-one will dent the value considerably – if you're not so bothered about originality, this could make a non-standard bike quite a bargain.

Over the years, the 750 lost power, later K models being a good 10mph slower than the earliest bikes, but were also smoother and quieter. Smoothest, quietest and slowest of all was the semi-automatic 750A. Adding a clutchless torque converter

750cc four still delivers decent performance.

two-speed transmission to the CB750 was intended to produce an easy-riding big bike. On sale from 1976, the CB750A was certainly that, but with its detuned engine and extra weight it was significantly slower than the conventional bike. They rarely come up for sale today, as only around 8000 were built, but it remains an intriguing aside to the story, and if you can find one, it would be an interesting bike to own.

Meanwhile, Honda had to do something to counter the new generation of four-cylinder 750s that were making the original CB look old-fashioned. So, it took the same route as the 400/4 and 550F, with a Super Sport version: four-into-one exhaust, slimmer fuel tank, lower bars and a small tailpiece. Power was back up to 67bhp, top speed to 115-120mph, and the frame geometry was changed to quicken the steering.

Unfortunately, the CB750F1 wasn't a great success, and that is reflected in its desirability today. Lower gearing boosted acceleration, but gave the bike a 35mpg thirst (and the smaller gearbox sprocket wore out the chain faster). That plus the smaller tank limited fuel range to 100 miles, while the geometry changes produced a scary straightline weave. The F2 of 1977 sought to address the criticisms with twin front discs, higher gearing, O-ring chain, new front forks and another geometry change to bring back stability. Comstar wheels and an all-black engine/gearbox are easy recognition points for the F2, which is generally preferred to the F1 and commands higher prices. There was a final F3 in 1978, with minor changes.

Strengths/weaknesses: The original Honda four remains the icon of the range, glamorous, reasonably fast and with real presence. Lots to choose from (except for rare K0 and CB750A). Brakes and handling not up to sports riding, a big bike that needs to be mastered.

CB750: 188%

Specials

For sporting riders of the 1970s who loved the Honda 750's power and stamina, but hated its heavy, wobbly chassis, there was an alternative. Several frame manufacturers offered kits or complete bikes to transform the Honda with better handling and lower weight.

The Seeley Hondas were probably the most successful, with 300 frames made between 1975 and 1978, most of them sold as kits. Both frame and swing arm were of Reynolds 531 tubing, with taper-roller steering head bearings. The result was 40lb lighter than a standard CB750, with a two-inch lower seat, a 4.5-gallon fuel tank (5.5-gallon with the optional solo seat) and the additional options of twin front disc brakes and Lester alloy wheels. They were sold in twelve countries. Seeley also offered the limited edition Honda CB750 Britain in 1978, based on the F2 with a big endurance style fairing, twin Cibie headlights, alloy fuel tank and Seeley's own exhaust.

Rickman's version was the CR750, which looked the part of a racer for the road, with clip-ons, rear-sets, a solo seat, slim upper fairing and a tailpiece. Dresda built batches of a road-going café racer in a long wheelbase frame, while Egli suspended the Honda engine in a trademark open-bottomed frame, with the Swiss tuner's own exhaust and cast wheels. Also worth looking out for is the 400/4-based Mocheck Harrier, a replica of the dealer's TT Formula Two racer, with single headlight fairing and Yoshimura 460cc conversion.

All of these specials are rare and command a premium price, though they rarely come up for sale. If you want one, check the bike's history carefully, as many have been raced.

5 Before you view
– be well informed

To avoid a wasted journey, and the disappointment of finding that the bike does not match your expectations, it will help if you're very clear about what questions you want to ask before you pick up the phone. Some of these points might appear basic, but when you're excited about the prospect of buying your dream classic, it's amazing how some of the most obvious things slip the mind. Also check the current values of the model in which you are interested in the classic bike magazine classified ads.

Where is the bike?
Is it going to be worth travelling to the next county/state, or even across a border? A locally advertised machine, although it may not sound very interesting, can add to your knowledge for very little effort, so make a visit – it might even be in better condition than expected.

Dealer or private sale?
Establish early on if the bike is being sold by its owner or by a trader. A private owner should have all the history, so don't be afraid to ask detailed questions. A dealer may have more limited knowledge of the bike's history, but should have some documentation. A dealer may offer a warranty/guarantee (ask for a printed copy).

Cost of collection and delivery?
A dealer may well be used to quoting for delivery. A private owner may agree to meet you halfway, but only agree to this after you have seen the bike at the vendor's address to validate the documents. Conversely, you could meet halfway and agree the sale, but insist on meeting at the vendor's address for the handover.

View – when and where?
It is always preferable to view at the vendor's home or business premises. In the case of a private sale, the bike's documentation should tally with the vendor's name and address. Arrange to view only in daylight, and avoid a wet day – the vendor may be reluctant to let you take a test ride if it's wet.

Reason for sale?
Do make it one of the first questions. Why is the bike being sold and how long has it been with the current owner? How many previous owners?

Condition?
Ask for an honest appraisal of the bike's condition. Ask specifically about some of the check items described in Chapter 8.

All original specification?
A completely original Honda four will be worth more than a modified one, but certain mods (such as electronic ignition) can also indicate a conscientious owner who has been actively riding/caring for the machine.

Matching data/legal ownership?

Do frame, engine numbers and licence plate match the official registration document? Is the owner's name and address recorded in the official registration documents?

For those countries that require an annual test of roadworthiness, does the bike have a document showing it complies (an MoT certificate in the UK, which can be verified on 0845 600 5977)?

If it's a 1973 or later bike, does it carry a current road fund licence/licence plate tag? Earlier bikes are road tax exempt in the UK.

Does the vendor own the bike outright? Money might be owed to a finance company or bank: the bike could even be stolen. Several organisations will supply the data on ownership, based on the bike's licence plate number, for a fee. Such companies can often also tell you whether the bike has been 'written off' by an insurance company. In the UK these organisations can supply vehicle data:

HPI – 01722 422 422 – www.hpicheck.com
AA – 0870 600 0836 – www.theaa.com
RAC – 0870 533 3660 – www.rac.co.uk
Other countries will have similar organisations.

Insurance

Check with your existing insurer before setting out – your current policy might not cover you if you do buy the bike and decide to ride it home.

How you can pay?

A cheque/check will take several days to clear and the seller may prefer to sell to a cash buyer. However, a banker's draft (a cheque issued by a bank) is as good as cash, but safer, so contact your own bank and become familiar with the formalities that are necessary to obtain one.

Buying at auction?

If the intention is to buy at auction see Chapter 10 for further advice.

Professional vehicle check (mechanical examination)

There are often marque/model specialists who will undertake professional examination of a vehicle on your behalf. Owners clubs may be able to put you in touch with such specialists.

6 Inspection equipment
– these items will really help

This book
Reading glasses (if you need them for close work)
Overalls
Digital camera
Compression tester
A friend, preferably a knowledgeable enthusiast

Before you rush out of the door, gather together a few items that will help as you work your way around the bike. This book is designed to be your guide at every step, so take it along and use the check boxes to help you assess each area of the bike you're interested in. Don't be afraid to let the seller see you using it.

Take your reading glasses if you need them to read documents and make close up inspections.

Be prepared to get dirty. Take along a pair of overalls, if you have them. A digital camera is handy so that later you can study some areas of the bike more closely. Take a picture of any part of the bike that causes you concern, and seek a friend's opinion.

A compression tester is handy if you have doubts about the engine's condition, though it will be tricky to access the inner two cylinders.

Ideally, have a friend or knowledgeable enthusiast accompany you; a second opinion is always valuable.

Appearance & engine

Put the bike on its centre stand, to shed equal light on both sides, and take a good, slow walk around it. If it's claimed to be restored, and has a nice shiny tank and engine cases, look more closely – how far does the 'restored' finish go? Are the nooks and crannies behind the gearbox as spotless as the fuel tank? If not, the bike may have been given a quick smarten up to sell. A generally faded look all over isn't necessarily a bad thing – it suggests a machine that hasn't been restored, and isn't trying to pretend that it has.

Now look at the engine – by far the most expensive and time-consuming thing to put right if anything's wrong. Contrary to what you may have heard, old Hondas do occasionally leak oil, but you shouldn't see anything more serious than a minor weep from the cylinder head to barrel joint.

Start the engine – it should fire up readily and rev up crisply and cleanly without showing

Cam chain adjuster may be butchered and bodged.

blue smoke from the exhaust. Listen carefully to the engine – Honda fours aren't especially quiet mechanically, so expect some rattling and rustling, but most of this should fade away as the engine warms up. Clutch rattle is inherent and not a sign of trouble – if the noise disappears when you pull in the clutch lever, then that's all it is. Any persistent rattling, or knocking from the bottom end, is the precursor to serious work. While the engine's running, check that the oil light has gone out.

Does the engine rattle persistently when warm?

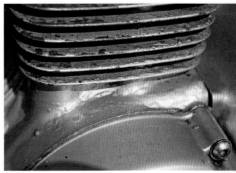

Bubbling lacquer is only a cosmetic problem, but expensive to put right.

Cycle parts

Switch off the engine and put the bike back on its centre stand. Check for play in the forks, headstock and swingarm. Are there leaks from the front forks or rear shocks? Check the wheels for loose or broken spokes, and run a screwdriver lightly over the spokes (which obviously doesn't apply to later bikes with Comstar wheels), listening for any that are 'off key'

Partially seized brake caliper is a common fault.

– these are the loose ones. Do the tyres have a decent amount of tread, or are they so old that they've gone hard and cracked? Check that the chain is well lubed and adjusted, and that the sprocket teeth aren't hooked.

Are details like the seat, badges and tank colour right for the year of the bike? (A little research helps here, and the reference books and websites listed at the end of this volume have all this information).

Documentation & numbers

If the seller claims to be the bike's owner, make sure he/she really is by checking the registration document, which in the UK is V5C. The person listed on the V5 isn't necessarily the legal owner, but their details should match those of whoever is selling the bike. Also use the V5C to check the engine/frame numbers, and that these match those on the bike – engine number is on top of the crankcase, frame number stamped onto steering head.

An annual roadworthiness certificate – the 'MoT' in the UK – is handy proof not just that the bike was roadworthy when tested, but a whole sheaf of them gives evidence of the bike's history – when it was actively being used, and what the mileage was. The more of these that come with the bike, the better.

VIN plate holds more information.

The engine and frame numbers are vital clues when investigating a bike's bona fides. First of all, check them against the seller's documentation, and if they don't match then walk away. Second, referring to the back of this book, check that they match with the model type, so that what you're looking at isn't a common or garden K2 CB750 masquerading as a rare K0. Even if the engine and frame numbers aren't original, the bike might still be worth buying if they match the documents, but that should be reflected in the price.

On four-into-four exhausts, check carefully for corrosion – they're more suseptible than the four-into-ones, as they run cooler and the condensation drain holes are easily blocked. Even if they look shiny on top, check at the bottom, near the front of the pipes.

Is the front brake dragging? If so, the caliper is partially or completely seized, and if the caliper piston and bore are badly pitted, you might even need a new (or decent secondhand) caliper.

Listen for noises, as detailed in Chapter 9. Rattles and knocks that persist in a warm engine (assuming they're not clutch rattle, which does no harm) are bad news – a reason to knock the price down if you're willing to tackle an engine overhaul, or to walk away if not. While looking at the engine, ask the owner how often he/she changes the oil and filter, and when the cam chain was last adjusted. Oil changes every 1500-2000 miles are a good sign.

Score each section as follows: 4 = excellent; 3 = good; 2 = average; 1 = poor
The totting up procedure is detailed at the end of the chapter. Be realistic in your marking!

Engine/frame numbers

Frame numbers are found on the steering head, and engine numbers on top of the crankcase. The exact postion varies between models – on 400s, for example, the frame number is stamped onto the right-hand side of the steering head, with a VIN plate riveted to the downtube, and the engine number is on top of the crankcase, viewed from the right-hand side – on the 750, look from the left-hand side.

Frame number is found on steering head.

There may also be a VIN plate.

Engine number on top of crankcase behind engine.

Honda fours aren't like certain classic British bikes, in which matching engine and frame numbers are the holy grail of an original machine. The engines and frames were actually made in different factories, so although the starting numbers were the same, they soon ran out of sequence, though they shouldn't differ by more than 2000 or so. If the numbers are way out, you may have mix 'n' match engine/frame. This isn't the end of the world – a non-orginal bike may still be a perfectly sound motorcycle, but the lack of originality needs to be reflected in the price.

Check engine and frame numbers against the model/year information in the back of this book, which should prove whether the bike is what it claims to be. Also check against the documentation.

Paint/chrome

Hondas have long been known for their good finish, and the paintwork on the fours confirms it – there are plenty of bikes around in their original coat of paint, which still polishes up well. Look out for scratches and chips – these aren't enough to reject any bike, but if unsightly they are a lever to reduce the price.

If a bike does need respraying or touching up, Honda doesn't supply the paint any more, so it's a case of finding the closest match possible with a modern shade. This is especially tricky with the Candy metallics, which used a base coat of silver followed by layers of coloured lacquer. These are very difficult to match, so if anything needs a respray it's probably best to have both tank and side panels repainted at the same time. To guide the sprayer, try to find an unworn section of paintwork (under the tank is often a good place), or an original colour brochure to pinpoint the original shade.

Frame paint lasts less well, and the only real way to achieve a concours finish is repainting (or better still, powder coating) the complete stripped frame.

Chrome work lasts well, but, as on any other bike, it will go dull and corrode if neglected, and on a 40-year-old bike it's unlikely to be pristine. The exhaust collector box goes first; it has thin chrome and tends to get overlooked at bike wash time. Before viewing the bike, check the prices of chrome parts that might need replacing – exhaust, wheel rims, etc – so you have an idea of what to bargain with.

Chips and scratches aren't a big problem unless you're buying a concours machine.

Blued chrome on the downpipes (these are fine) indicate aftermarket pipes.

Crazing will need a respray to put right.

Original chrome generally lasts well.

Check the tank for dents and scratches.

Mudguards should be rust- and dent-free.

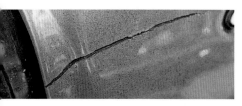

Plastic panels can crack.

Some badges are still available.

Tinwork

One advantage of buying an old motorcycle, as opposed to an old car, is that there's far less bodywork to worry about, and on the Honda fours this amounts to the fuel tank, plastic side panels (and on some F models, tailpiece) and mudguards.

Few of these are available new, though you might be lucky and find some old unused stock, but there are plenty of sound or restorable secondhand items, if the ones on the bike you're looking at really are beyond repair. Rear mudguards for the 400 or 750 for example, can't be bought new, but refurbished old ones are offered by one specialist for around £200. Because so many Honda fours of all types were made, it's unlikely that you'll be absolutely stuck for a part.

Check the fuel tank for dents and scratches, and that the lockable filler cap (if fitted) works as it should. The plastic side panel mountings can snap off if the panel is prised off the wrong way (a common mistake), but these can be repaired with epoxy resin. The panels also crack, which again is repairable, with care, using a glassfibre patch on the back to strengthen the panel, though of course it will need repainting afterwards – note the above comments on paint matching. Check the mudguards for corrosion (not just of the surface chrome, but the steel beneath), and factor in the cost of replacements as a bargaining tool.

Badges

Badges and transfers are often unavailable for older Japanese bikes, but some of these are on offer, including tank badges for the 750 and side panel transfers for the 400. The 400/4 was the only bike to use transfers for fuel tank as well as side panels, while the 350, 500 and 750 K bikes all had metal badges on both tank and panels. In each case,

Others are hard to find.

400/4 used transfers on the side panels.

check that the badges/transfers aren't broken or missing, and it helps if you know whether replacements are available before viewing the bike.

Seat

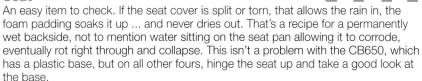

An easy item to check. If the seat cover is split or torn, that allows the rain in, the foam padding soaks it up ... and never dries out. That's a recipe for a permanently wet backside, not to mention water sitting on the seat pan allowing it to corrode, eventually rot right through and collapse. This isn't a problem with the CB650, which has a plastic base, but on all other fours, hinge the seat up and take a good look at the base.

If the seat isn't resting evenly on the frame tubes of a 750, it's probably because previous owners have been using the seat as a lifting handle when hoiking the bike up onto its centre stand, bending the seat pan in the process. The answer is to use the grab handle which Honda thoughtfully provided to prevent that happening.

Some new seats are available (though 500/550 items are hard to find), and the good news is that Honda didn't change the style much, which makes life simpler. A cheaper solution is to have the existing seat recovered (and if necesssary, the pan rewelded) by a specialist. That's simpler still on the 650, whose plastic base

means a new cover can just be stapled on. Pattern seats are another alternative. Beware the appearance of a humped seat on the 400/4 – the standard item had only the suggestion of a hump, and anything larger is an aftermarket seat bolted on.

A seat should be free of splits and tears.

Non-standard seats (like this one) adversely affect value.

Rubbers [4] [3] [2] [1]

Worn footrest rubbers are a sign of high mileage, though as they're so cheap and easy to replace, not an infallible one. They should be secure on the footrest and free of splits or tears. If the footrest itself is bent upwards, that's a sure sign the bike has been down the road at some point, so look for other telltale signs on that side. The kickstart and gearchange rubbers are also easy to replace, so well worn ones could indicate owner neglect. Not

Worn rubbers indicate high mileage.

that the kickstart should have had much use, as Honda electrics are pretty reliable – nevertheless, all sohc fours apart from the 650 were equipped with one.

Frame [4] [3] [2] [1]

No surprises here. All these Honda fours used thoroughly conventional tubular steel frames, semi-double cradle on the 350 and 400 (ie a single front downtube splitting into two half way down) and a full double cradle (twin downtubes from headstock to engine mountings) on all the others.

None have any particular weaknesses, though that of the 750 struggled to cope at high cornering speeds, which was why so many frame specialists offered stiffer, lighter alternatives, to make full use of engine power. That said, even the 750 frame is perfectly adequate for brisk touring, so at normal road speeds it's not really a problem.

It's easy to overlook the finish on a frame, dominated as it is by

Check the steering head for damage.

Non-original paint on this frame is rough around the edges.

flashier paint, chrome and a big alloy engine. But take a close peek – if the paint is flaking off and rust showing through, then it's a big job to put right, necessitating a complete stripdown of the whole bike. On the other hand, there's a lot to be said for leaving a faded frame just as it is, if it fits in with the overall patina of the bike – a newly repainted or recoated frame can make the rest of the bike look shabby!

The most important job is to check whether the main frame is straight and true. Crash damage may have bent it, putting the wheels out of line. One way of checking is with an experienced eye, string and a straight edge, but the surest way to ascertain a frame's straightness is on the test ride – any serious

Crashbars are non-original, but help prevent crash damage.

misalignment should be obvious in the way the bike handles. Consistently pulling to one side is a sure sign that either the frame or forks are bent. Also examine the steering head for damage, which is evidence of a head-on collision.

Stands

All bikes were equipped with both centre and side stands, and these work pretty well. When looking at the bike, pull it up onto the centre stand and then try rocking it from side to side – there should be no movement at all. If there is, the stand will need a weld repair – not difficult, but another bargaining counter. Similarly with the side stand, check that this is secure both on the bike and when holding it up.

The side stand should not be wobbly ...

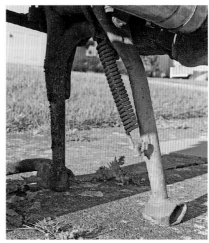

... nor should the centre stand.

Lights

4 3 2 1

By the standards of the time, these Hondas had pretty good lights, supplied by reliable 12-volt electrics. But in the early 21st century, no one will be impressed by the 750's 40/50w headlight, let alone the 350's 35/50. Fortunately, they can be upgraded, right up to an 80/100w headlight where local laws allow. Don't forget to check that the lights work – if none of them do, then the relevant fuse is the problem, otherwise if just one light isn't working, then it's a bulb.

Most bikes used this style of rear light.

Headlights aren't brilliant by modern standards.

Electrics/wiring

4 3 2 1

We've already mentioned the decent electrics fitted to all of these Hondas, and it's worth reiterating. The 12-volt alternator is extremely reliable, and unlike some classic bikes has power in hand. Having said that, components will fail over time – rectifiers and coils will eventually give up; batteries lose their charge and capacity to hold it if left unused for a long time, which many of these bikes are. And don't forget that the youngest of these bikes is now over 25 years old, so the original wiring and connectors will be past their best.

Check that everything works – starter, lights, indicators, horn, warning lights – and take a look at any exposed wiring (under the seat and around the steering head). Any signs of untidy bodged repairs are bad news. Many electrical problems are simply caused by poor connections or bad earths, so if you're handy with a multi-meter, an electrically malfunctioning Honda could be the makings of a bargain.

Many of these fours suffer from wet electrics, with ignition coils exposed to the weather, leading to inevitable misfires in the rain. The coils can be relocated to a more weatherproof spot, so ask if the owner has done this. On 400/4s, the problem was compounded by metal plug cap covers that trapped water, again causing misfires – most have these have probably been removed by now. If the bike is misfiring on one

Misfiring is usually caused by wet electrics.

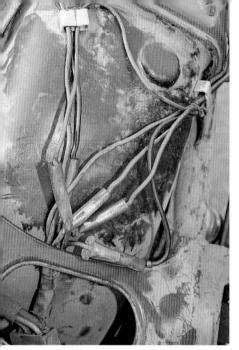

Check the wiring hasn't been bodged.

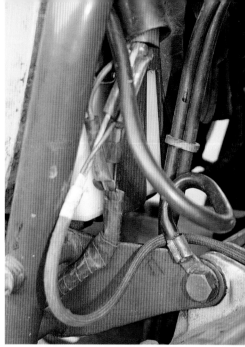

Faults are often caused by no more than a bad earth.

They all came with indicators – do these work?

or more cylinders in the dry, then an ignition fault is mostly likely – suspect the points (apart from the 650, which had electronic ignition), plugs or coils.

CB750 alternator leads can come loose, which upsets charging, and a few 400s have a strange fusebox fault that allows the 15-amp fuse to overheat and fail. If the lights aren't working, that's likely to be the cause. No one knows why this happens, and the only insurance is a few spare fuses.

Wheels/tyres [4] [3] [2] [1]

Apart from the CB650 and late 750s with their Comstar wheels, all the fours used spoked wheels with chromed steel rims. Check that the chrome is intact and not pitted or peeling away. The standard chrome holds up fairly well, but if you need new rims, DID still make them. Run a screwdriver lightly over the spokes – any that sound 'off' will need tensioning. If any spokes are broken or missing, the bike is unrideable. Watch for this on the CB750 rear wheel in particular.

The smaller fours are not especially hard on tyres, but it's a different matter with the 750, whose weight and power give the tyres a much harder time. If the tyre is worn, the legal minimum in the UK is at least 1mm of tread depth across at least

The wheel rim should look like this!

three-quarters of the breadth of the tyre. Something else to consider is that most of these bikes cover very few miles each year, and the tyres may be many years old. Eventually, they will harden and crack, losing their grip in the process – try sticking a fingernail into the tyre. If the rubber is too hard to leave an impression, budget on a new set of rubber. All the fours use 18- or 19-inch wheels (apart from the final K7 750, which used a 17-inch rear), so there's a good choice of modern tyres.

Check tyres for cracking and hardness as well as tread wear.

Wheel bearings

4 3 2 1

Honda fours aren't especially hard on wheel bearings, and the bits themselves aren't expensive. However, fitting them is a hassle, and badly worn bearings could affect handling, so it's worth checking them out. Put the bike on its centre stand, and with

the steering on full lock try rocking the front wheel in a vertical plane, then spin the wheel and listen for signs of roughness.

Now grasp the rear wheel (which should be clear of the ground) and do the same for that one, but don't mistake movement at the swing arm pivot for wheel bearing play, though either way, it's bad news. If the wheel rim is moving in relation to the hub (on front or rear wheel) then you have a serious spoke problem.

Play should be obvious when checked.

Steering head bearings 4 3′ 2 1

Again, the bearings don't cost an arm or leg, but trouble here can affect the handling, and changing them is a big job. With the bike on the centre stand and the front wheel clear of the ground, swing the handlebars from lock to lock. They should move freely, with not a hint of roughness or stiff patches – if there is, budget for replacing the bearings. To check for play, take the bike off the centre stand, hold the front brake on and try to rock the bike back and forth, or with the bike on the stand, grab the bottom of the fork legs and try rocking these.

The ball bearings on the CB750 are particularly prone to digging in, as they're not really up to the bike's weight. This leads to an odd, notchy feel to the steering. The answer (and this will improve the handling of any Honda four) is a set of taper-roller bearings – if an owner has done this (or paid someone else to do it) that's a good sign of a keen and conscientious rider.

Worn steering head bearings affect the handling.

Swing arm bearings 4 3 2 1

Yet again, a simple bearing check, but absolutely vital, as even minor wear can have a bad effect on handling. Honda often fitted plastic bearings as standard, which

aren't a problem until they start to wear. A far superior replacement are phosphor bronze bushes, which will last longer if kept regularly greased, and give more precise handling in the first place. As with the taper-roller steering head, this is a sign of a caring owner.

To check the swing arm pivot bearings, rock the rear wheel as you did for the wheel bearing check, and if there is any movement, try to ascertain whether it's coming from the wheel hub, or up at the swing arm. Alternatively, grasp the rear of the swing arm and try rocking that, though movement is harder to check here than at the wheel rim.

Don't forget to check the swing arm bearings as well.

Suspension

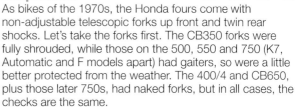

As bikes of the 1970s, the Honda fours come with non-adjustable telescopic forks up front and twin rear shocks. Let's take the forks first. The CB350 forks were fully shrouded, while those on the 500, 550 and 750 (K7, Automatic and F models apart) had gaiters, so were a little better protected from the weather. The 400/4 and CB650, plus those later 750s, had naked forks, but in all cases, the checks are the same.

To check the fork bushes, take the bike off its stand, hold the front brake on and pump the forks up and down. They should move smoothly and without clonking, and any play in the bushes should be obvious, though don't confuse it with play in the steering head bearings. An alternative method is to grasp the bottom of the forks with the bike on its centre stand, and try to rock them back and forth.

Now look at the stanchions. Any oil leaks will be obvious on naked forks, but if there are gaiters, try rubbing them on the stanchion – if one moves more easily than the other, there's a leak. On 750s, the answer is to use the later type

Shrouded forks on the CB350/4.

Check stanchions for leaks and pitting.

Bouncy rear shocks will need replacing.

Check fork bushes for play.

double-lip seal. If the stanchions are pitted, they'll need replacing. Genuine new ones are available for some bikes, but they're not cheap. Fortunately, the originals can be reclaimed by grinding smooth, replating with hard chrome and regrinding to size. Specialists can do this.

The rear shocks can only really be checked on the test ride – seek out a few mid-corner bumps, on which any lack of damping should be obvious as the bike bounces a few times after the bump before settling again. As with the forks, check the shocks for leaks. The original Showa shocks are no longer available, but there are good quality pattern items.

Instruments

All fours, apart from the 750 Automatic, offered the same basic set of instruments, and these are fairly reliable. If they have failed (and a speedometer cable is more likely to be the culprit than an internal problem), then there are instrument specialists who can repair and rebuild them. The instrument faces fade over time, but the Vintage Japanese Motorcycle Club UK branch has specialists which can supply refurbished faces, though not for all models. It might sound like a small point, but for an otherwise immaculate bike, like-new instruments are the finishing touch.

Are the instrument faces faded or the lenses cracked?

Instruments can be refurbished, as here.

Engine/gearbox – general impression

The good news is that these are basically tough engines that can run to very high mileages without much trouble. In fact, the actual mileage is less important than how well the bike has been cared for. A Honda four given frequent oil/filter changes (with quality lube of the correct type), and regular camchain adjustment will indeed give a long, trouble-free life, but they will deteriorate if neglected.

This is something that's difficult to tell from just looking at the bike, but there are a few clues. A generally mucky and dirty engine is a sign of neglect, and note that oil weeps from the cylinder head joint will attract dirt, so keep a look-out for that. Have a closer look at the various fixings – the Phillips-head screws are quite soft and easily damaged; the sign of an impatient or ham-fisted owner. If you're not bothered about ultimate originality, then allen screws make good replacements.

General appearance can give some clues to engine condition.

A well restored engine on a well restored bike.

There may be weep leak.

Don't forget to have a look at the gearbox.

Also look out for rounded off nuts and bolts, especially on the oil filter housing. This is held in place by a small 12mm bolt that doesn't take kindly to ill-fitting spanners or (heaven help us) Mole grips. An aftermarket conversion to a 17mm bolt is a good sign that the bike's been looked after (certainly better than a rounded-off original).

You may not have heard the engine run yet, but on 400/4s you may still be able to tell something about the condition of the camchain. The adjuster is a small 6mm bolt plus locknut, mounted right at the front of the engine, and vulnerable to weather. If not cleaned and greased (or used for its intended purpose) regularly, this will seize up, and the next time someone tries to use it, snap off. One common response is to drill out the old part and use a bigger 10mm item, but the tensioner can then only be adjusted by removing a blanking plug and poking a screwdriver down the hole, which moves the tensioner and tightens the camchain. If the bike has been bodged like this, walk away, or negotiate a lower price. Ironically, adjusting the cam chain tension with an intact adjustment bolt is simplicity itself – with the engine idling, slacken the locknut. The tensioner then automatically adjusts itself, and you retighten the locknut.

Some Honda fours do leak oil from the cylinder head joint. It's rare, but both the 400 and 750 are affected. The cure for the 400/4 is a new Honda gasket that glues itself to both head and barrel from engine heat after the first start-up. On 750s, head leakage only usually affects pre-'74 bikes – from engine number CB750E 2352923, it was recitified. Also on 750s, check for leaks around the gearbox sprocket – this could be just a maladjusted chain oiler on early bikes, or (more seriously) the oil seal behind the sprocket not doing its job.

Finally on this initial engine inspection, ask whether electronic ignition has been fitted (all bikes except the CB650 had contact breaker points as standard). Unless you want a bike that is original even in the bits you can't see, this is a worthwhile modification to have, giving easier starting and smoother running.

Engine – starting/idling

All but the very late fours have both electric and kickstart – the latter is largely superfluous, given the bikes' reliable electrics and starter motors, though the 400's kickstart can break. This can be rewelded, but it takes an expert to do it.

The engine should start promptly.

Hot or cold, the engine should fire up on the electric start immediately, though it will take a while to warm up from cold, with careful use of the manual choke. Reluctance to start could be down to a whole host of factors: weak battery and dirty fuel system (if the bike has been standing), or plugs and points that need adjusting/replacing. It's likely to be a relatively simple fault, but you do need to hear the engine running properly to make a decision! (Unless of course the price reflects a non-running condition.)

Carburettor balance is the key to smooth, even running.

The idle should be smooth and even – if it's lumpy and uneven, then out-of-balance carburettors are the most likely cause. All the fours have one carb per cylinder, and each carb slide has to open in exact unison with the other three. Early 750s, without the later lifting shaft, are more prone to this, but rebalancing the carbs is a relatively simple job with the aid of a set of vacuum gauges. Check the lifting shaft for wear or stiffness, and also the lifting rod for each carb slide by rocking them. Each rod should have the same amount of axial play. If the engine appears to be running unevenly, place a hand under (but not on!) each exhaust pipe in turn – if one is cooler than the others, then that cylinder isn't firing properly (or at all).

Engine – smoke/noise

Now get down close to the engine and have a listen. The Honda fours are mechanically quite noisy, but they should quieten down as the engine warms up – if a top end rattle persists, then it's likely to be the cam chain, its tensioner, or the camshaft bearings themselves. The smaller fours' cam runs directly in the head, the bigger fours in carrier bearings – it's an engine-out job to replace on the 750. Top end wear is usually the result of oil running low, or not being changed often enough. Ask when the camchain was last adjusted, because it could be that simple. If it's allowed to run slack, it will eventually start cutting into the cylinder block, throwing swarf into the rest of the engine. Similarly, a neglected tensioner will eventually start to break up, depositing particles of rubber. Cam chains and tensioners can last 60,000 miles on a cared-for engine.

But don't confuse cam chain rattle with clutch rattle. All the fours have this, which is inherent and does no harm at all – if the noise disappears when you pull the clutch

Listen for camchain rattle on the 400/4.

lever in, then that's what it is. Balancing the carbs will also minimise clutch rattle.

A knocking from the bottom end of the engine at idle is more likely to be the primary chain than worn main bearings, but it still involves a complete engine strip. A worn primary will also show up as roughness and slack in the transmission – if the final drive chain is in good condition, then the primary is likely to be at fault.

Expect some mechanical noise, but not persistent rattles when warm.

Now blip the throttle and watch for blue smoke. The Honda fours aren't habitual oil burners, and shouldn't use oil when all is well. Blue smoke usually just means it's time for new piston rings, or new pistons and a rebore if the wear is serious. Cared-for engines can run to 40,000 miles before a rebore is due. Do check the oil level – on 400s, blue smoke is sometimes a result of the sump being over-filled.

And watch for blue smoke.

Rarer engine faults include dropped valves on the 400/4, but since it is rare, and there's no warning, it's not really worth worrying about. The final CB750F2 is prone to burning valves if the clearances aren't checked and adjusted as they should be – watch for poor starting and flat performance.

Finally, if the engine sounds flat and rough, it could be that (and this is another rare one) the ignition auto-advance unit has been damaged if the bike has gone down hard on the right-hand side. If in doubt take off the timing cover, and with the engine idling, watch the ignition cam nut – if it's wobbling, then the auto advance has been bent and needs replacing.

Chain/sprockets

With the engine switched off, examine the final drive chain and sprockets. Is the chain clean, well lubed and properly adjusted? The best way to check its wear is to

Check chain for wear, adjustment and lube.

Hooked teeth means new sprockets needed.

take hold of a link and try to pull it rearwards away from the sprocket. It should only reveal a small portion of the sprocket teeth – any more, and it needs replacing.

Check the rear sprocket teeth for wear – if they have a hooked appearance, the sprocket needs replacing. Ditto if any teeth are damaged or missing. And if the rear sprocket needs replacing, then the gearbox sprocket will too. Chain and sprockets aren't massively expensive, but changing the gearbox sprocket takes some dismantling time.

The 750's chain in particular has a hard time, and it isn't unknown (though rare) for a chain to snap on the big bike and punch a hole in the crankcase. But a properly lubed and adjusted chain won't give a problem.

Battery

Hinge up the seat, or remove the left-hand side panel, and check the battery. Acid splashes indicate overcharging. The correct electrolyte level is a good sign of a meticulous owner, and do check that the battery is secured in place by its rubber strap. If it can jump around, this strains the cables and it might short out.

The battery should be secure and well topped-up.

Exhaust

Always an objection of fascination on any Honda four, whether it's the sinuous four-into-one of the 400/4 or 550F, or the look-at-me four-piper fitted to the 500 and 750 K models.

The four-into-fours are prone to corrosion, as they have a large surface area which runs cooler and develops condensation, especially on short journeys. Honda provided little drain holes, but these clog with road dirt (and on the left-hand side, chain lube). Check the system underneath at its lowest point, as this is where the rust starts. Unless you want complete

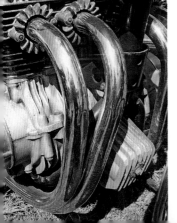

Check downpipes for rust and blueing.

Collector box on 4-into-1 exhausts is the first part to corrode.

Downpipe clamps must be tight and secure.

originality, a four-into-one replacement is a good idea, as it'll be lighter, cheaper and run hotter.

Because of the cost of genuine exhausts, many owners have opted for an aftermarket four-into-one, such as the Motad. Some of these are quality items, but they will detract from the bike's value. The other problem with pattern systems is that they have single-skinned downpipes, which soon start to blue – the Honda parts are double-skinned.

On 400/4s, check the collector box for corrosion, as this fails first. At the time of writing, Honda will only supply complete 400/4 systems, though some specialists may be prepared to split the system and just sell you what you need.

Test ride
The test ride should be not less than 15 minutes, and you should be doing the riding – not the seller riding with you on the pillion. It's understandable that some sellers are reluctant to let a complete stranger loose on their pride and joy, but it does go with the territory of selling a bike, and so long as you leave an article of faith (usually the vehicle you arrived in) then all should be happy. Take your driving licence in case the seller wants to see it.

Main warning lights
There are four or five main warning lights – indicators, oil, neutral and main beam. Check that they all work, but the crucial one is the oil light, this should go out as soon as the engine fires up. If it doesn't, the bike is low on oil or the engine is seriously worn.

These clusters are now available new.

Early warning light clusters.

All engines should pull evenly through the rev range.

But don't expect lots of midrange torque from the smaller fours.

A clutch in good condition won't slip or drag.

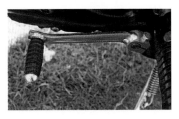

Gears should engage cleanly and stay there.

Engine performance

The Honda fours' rideability might not be up to modern standards, but they're still pretty good. All of them should pull smoothly from low speeds, without hesitation or any jerks and graunches from the transmission. Don't expect instant grunt from the little 350 and 400, but the 650 and 750 should deliver a decent pull from low revs. All engines should pull smoothly right through the rev range, without misfiring or flat spots – in either case, an ignition fault is the most likely cause.

Don't abuse the bike on the test ride, but if road conditions allow, it is worth one run in a lower gear up to the red line. When you get back, check that the hot engine is still idling nice and evenly.

Clutch operation

Make a note of how the clutch feels. That on the CB500 can be stiff unless the mechanism and cable are in absolutely tiptop condition. The 550 was better. On all bikes, the clutch is generally reliable and shouldn't slip or drag. It's also easy to adjust via an access hole on the outer casing. If the clutch is slipping, it could just be that the owner is using the wrong oil. On all these bikes, the clutch/gearbox share the same oil as the engine, which should be 10/40 or 15/40, not 20/50. A slipping clutch on a 750 could be a sign of general wear, in which case new plates are the answer.

Gearbox operation

Some contemporary tests criticised the Honda fours for notchy gearchanges, others praised their smoothness – take your pick! The important point on the test ride is to check that the gears are reasonably quiet, engage properly, and don't jump out of engagement.

The 750 is sometimes afflicted with this latter problem, especially in third and fourth – try accelerating, then decelerating in each gear to check for jumping out. It can be cured with new gears, but that means removing the engine from the frame. On the 400/4, sixth gear is the one to watch, in this case for noise. If the mainshaft and/or countershaft are worn, it will grind rather than give the normal whine, and there may be bits of of shaft sitting in the sump. Otherwise, these Honda gearboxes are pretty reliable and trouble-free – as with the engine, it's running on low oil that causes problems.

Handling

Big differences here, depending on which bike you're riding. The original 400/4 was rightly praised as the best handling Honda ever (at the time) and it really is a whole load of fun, being light, flickable and secure. The other small and middleweight fours aren't quite as good, but they're still fun to ride, and all are improved by modern tyres. The 750 has its limitations, and can be intimidating if you're not used to a big, heavy bike, though it's still perfectly adequate for touring rather than sports riding.

In all cases, check that the bike runs happily in a straight line without pulling to one side. In the corners, there's no need to try and touch down footrests on the test ride, but the bike shouldn't wallow or feel vague when banked over – if it does, worn shocks and/or forks, steering head bearings or swing arm bearings will be at fault.

Brakes

Brakes are an achilles heel for the Honda fours. As standard, the CB750 K model's single front disc was marginal to cope with the bike's weight and performance, especially in modern traffic conditions. This was compounded by the stainless steel disc Honda fitted, which didn't rust, but didn't work too well in the wet either. A replacement disc and modern pads improve matters greatly, and brakes on the smaller fours are adequate in standard form.

The real problem lies in the aluminium swinging caliper fitted to all but the very late bikes. This pivots on a steel pin, and seizes onto it if the assembly isn't cleaned and regreased regularly, especially on bikes used through the winter or left standing for long periods. Try pushing the bike around – if the front brake is dragging, then the caliper is sticking. Caliper pistons can also corrode but new pistons and seal kits are available. The rear drum brake fitted to

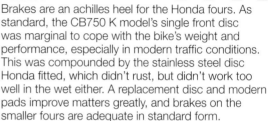

The rear drum works well ...

... but the front disc is less well thought of.

Modern pads and discs will make a big difference.

If brakes are dragging, the caliper is the problem.

many of these bikes is trouble-free. On the test ride, check that both brakes work smoothly, without binding.

Also check that the bleed nipple on the caliper is in place, as it seizes in place and snaps off very easily. The only way to remove the remains is to drill them out.

Check cables work smoothly.

Cables

All the control cables – throttle and choke – should work smoothly without stiffness or jerking. Poorly lubricated, badly adjusted cables are an indication of general neglect, and the same goes for badly routed cables.

Switchgear

All bikes used the same basic switchgear, familiar to anyone who has ridden a 1970s Japanese bike. They are reliable and decent quality, but still check that everything works as it should. If anything does go wrong, or they are past repair, new ones are available in most cases.

No real problems here, but check everything works.

Some new switches are available.

Evaluation procedure
Add up the total points.
Score: 120 = excellent; 90 = good; 60 = average; 30 = poor.

Bikes scoring over 84 will be completely useable and will require only maintenance and care to preserve condition. Bikes scoring between 30 and 61 will require serious restoration (at much the same cost regardless of score). Bikes scoring between 62 and 83 will require very careful assessment of necessary repair/restoration costs in order to arrive at a realistic value.

10 Auctions
– sold! Another way to buy your dream

Auction pros & cons
Pros:
Prices will usually be lower than those of dealers or private sellers and you might grab a real bargain on the day. Auctioneers have usually established clear title with the seller. At the venue you can usually examine documentation relating to the bike.

Cons:
You have to rely on a sketchy catalogue description of condition and history. The opportunity to inspect is limited and you cannot ride the bike. Auction machines can be a little below par and may require some work. It's easy to overbid. There will usually be a buyer's premium to pay in addition to the auction hammer price.

Which auction?
Auctions by established auctioneers are advertised in the motorcycle magazines and on the auction houses' websites. A catalogue, or a simple printed list of the lots for auctions might only be available a day or two ahead, though often lots are listed and pictured on auctioneers' websites much earlier. Contact the auction company to ask if previous auction selling prices are available as this is useful information (details of past sales are often available on websites).

Catalogue, entry fee and payment details
When you purchase the catalogue of the bikes in the auction, it often acts as a ticket allowing two people to attend the viewing days and the auction. Catalogue details tend to be comparatively brief, but will include information such as 'one owner from new, low mileage, full service history', etc. It will also usually show a guide price to give you some idea of what to expect to pay and will tell you what is charged as a 'Buyer's premium'. The catalogue will also contain details of acceptable forms of payment. At the fall of the hammer an immediate deposit is usually required, the balance payable within 24 hours. If the plan is to pay by cash there may be a cash limit. Some auctions will accept payment by debit card. Sometimes credit or charge cards are acceptable, but will often incur an extra charge. A bank draft or bank transfer will have to be arranged in advance with your own bank as well as with the auction house. No bike will be released before all payments are cleared. If delays occur in payment transfers then storage costs can accrue.

Buyer's premium
A buyer's premium will be added to the hammer price: don't forget this in your calculations. It is not usual for there to be a further state tax or local tax on the purchase price and/or on the buyer's premium.

Viewing
In some instances it's possible to view on the day, or days before, as well as in the hours prior to, the auction. There are auction officials available who are willing to help out if need be. While the officials may start the engine for you, a test ride is

out of the question. Crawling under and around the bike as much as you want is permitted. You can also ask to see any documentation available.

Bidding
Before you take part in the auction, decide your maximum bid – and stick to it!

It may take a while for the auctioneer to reach the lot you are interested in, so use that time to observe how other bidders behave. When it's the turn of your bike, attract the auctioneer's attention and make an early bid. The auctioneer will then look to you for a reaction every time another bid is made. Usually the bids will be in fixed increments until the bidding slows, when smaller increments will often be accepted before the hammer falls. If you want to withdraw from the bidding, make sure the auctioneer understands your intentions – a vigorous shake of the head when he or she looks to you for the next bid should do the trick!

Assuming that you are the successful bidder, the auctioneer will note your card or paddle number, and from that moment on you will be responsible for the bike.

If it is unsold, either because it failed to reach the reserve or because there was little interest, it may be possible to negotiate with the owner, via the auctioneers, after the sale is over.

Successful bid
There are two more items to think about – how to get the bike home, and insurance. If you can't ride it, your own or a hired trailer is one way, another is to have it shipped using the facilities of a local company. The auction house will also have details of companies specialising in the transport of bikes.

Insurance for immediate cover can usually be purchased on site, but it may be more cost-effective to make arrangements with your own insurance company in advance, and then call to confirm the full details.

eBay & other online auctions?
eBay & other online auctions could land you a Honda at a bargain price, though you'd be foolhardy to bid without examining it first, something most vendors encourage. A useful feature of eBay is that the geographical location of the bike is shown, so you can narrow your choices to those within a realistic radius of home. Be prepared to be outbid in the last few moments of the auction. Remember, your bid is binding and that it will be very, very difficult to get restitution in the case of a crooked vendor fleecing you – caveat emptor!

Be aware that some bikes offered for sale in online auctions are 'ghost' machines. Don't part with any cash without being sure that the vehicle does actually exist and is as described (usually pre-bidding inspection is possible).

Auctioneers

Bonhams	www.bonhams.com
British Car Auctions (BCA)	www.bca-europe.com or www.british-car-auctions.co.uk
Cheffins	www.cheffins.co.uk
DVCA	www.dvca.co.uk
eBay	www.ebay.com
H&H	www.classic-auctions.co.uk
Shannons	www.shannons.com.au
Silver	www.silverauctions.com

11 Paperwork
– correct documentation is essential!

The paper trail
Classic bikes sometimes come with a large portfolio of paperwork accumulated and passed on by a succession of proud owners. This documentation represents the real history of the machine, from which you can deduce how well it's been cared for, how much it's been used, which specialists have worked on it and the dates of major repairs and restorations. All of this information will be priceless to you as the new owner, so be very wary of bikes with little paperwork to support their claimed history.

Registration documents
All countries/states have some form of registration for private vehicles whether its like the American 'pink slip' system or the British 'log book' system.

It is essential to check that the registration document is genuine, that it relates to the bike in question, and that all the details are correctly recorded, including frame and engine numbers (if these are shown). If you are buying from the previous owner, his or her name and address will be recorded in the document: this will not be the case if you are buying from a dealer.

In the UK the current (Euro-aligned) registration document is the V5C, and is printed in coloured sections of blue, green and pink. The blue section relates to the motorcycle specification, the green section has details of the registered keeper (who is not necessarily the legal owner) and the pink section is sent to the DVLA in the UK when the bike is sold. A small section in yellow deals with selling within the motor trade.

In the UK the DVLA will provide details of earlier keepers of the bike upon payment of a small fee, and much can be learned in this way.

If the bike has a foreign registration there may be expensive and time-consuming formalities to complete. Do you really want the hassle? It is worth it if the bike you hanker after is more easily found abroad. USA buyers for example, are far more likely to find an original 400/4 in Europe (especially the UK) than at home, while UK buyers will find a much wider choice of 750s across the Atlantic.

However, you'll have to buy the bike sight unseen, and the paperwork involved in importing and re-registering is a daunting prospect. That means employing a shipping agent; you'll also have to budget in the shipping costs. Then there's (at the time of writing) 6% import duty on the bike and shipping costs, then 17.5% VAT on the whole lot. With a reasonable choice of Honda fours in most countries, it's not really worth the hassle.

Roadworthiness certificate
Most country/state administrations require that bikes are regularly tested to prove that they are safe to use on the public highway. In the UK that test (the 'MoT') is carried out at approved testing stations, for a fee. In the USA the requirement varies, but most states insist on an emissions test every two years as a minimum, whilst the police are charged with pulling over unsafe-looking vehicles.

In the UK the test is required on an annual basis for any bike over three years old. Of particular relevance for older bikes is that the certificate issued includes the mileage reading recorded at the test date and, therefore, becomes an independent record of that machine's history. Ask the seller if previous certificates are available. Without an MoT the vehicle should be trailered to its new home, unless you insist that a valid MoT is part of the deal. (Not such a bad idea this, as at least you will know the bike was roadworthy on the day it was tested and you don't need to wait for the old certificate to expire before having the test done.)

Road licence

The administration of every country/state charges some kind of tax for the use of its road system, the actual form of the 'road licence' and, how it is displayed, varying enormously country to country and state to state.

Whatever the form of the road licence, it must relate to the vehicle carrying it and must be present and valid if the bike is to be ridden on the public highway legally. The value of the licence will depend on the length of time it will continue to be valid.

In the UK if a bike is untaxed because it has not been used for a period of time, the owner has to inform the licencing authorities, otherwise the vehicle's date-related registration number will be lost and there will be a painful amount of paperwork to get it re-registered. Also in the UK, bikes built before the end of 1972 are exempt from road tax, but they must still display a valid disc. Bike clubs can often provide formal proof that a particular machine qualifies for this valuable concession.

Certificates of authenticity

For many makes of classic bike it is possible to get a certificate proving the age and authenticity (e.g. engine and frame numbers, paint colour and trim) of a particular machine. These are sometimes called 'Heritage Certificates' and if the bike comes with one of these it is a definite bonus. If you want to obtain one, the owners club is the best starting point.

Valuation certificate

Hopefully, the vendor will have a recent valuation certificate, or letter signed by a recognised expert stating how much he, or she, believes the particular bike to be worth (such documents, together with photos, are usually needed to get 'agreed value' insurance). Generally such documents should act only as confirmation of your own assessment of the bike rather than a guarantee of value as the expert has probably not seen it in the flesh. The easiest way to find out how to obtain a formal valuation is to contact the owners club.

Service history

Often these bikes will have been serviced at home by enthusiastic (and hopefully capable) owners for a good number of years. Nevertheless, try to obtain as much service history and other paperwork pertaining to the bike as you can. Naturally specialist garage receipts score most points in the value stakes. However, anything helps in the great authenticity game, items like the original bill of sale, handbook, parts invoices and repair bills, adding to the story and the character of the machine. Even a brochure correct to the year of the bike's manufacture is a useful document and something that you could well have to search hard to locate in future years. If the seller claims that the bike has been restored, then expect receipts and other evidence from a specialist restorer.

If the seller claims to have carried out regular servicing, ask what work was completed, when, and seek some evidence of it being carried out. Your assessment of the bike's overall condition should tell you whether the seller's claims are genuine.

Restoration photographs

If the seller tells you that the bike has been restored, then expect to be shown a series of photographs taken while the restoration was under way. Pictures taken at various stages, and from various angles, should help you gauge the thoroughness of the work. If you buy the bike, ask if you can have all the photographs as they form an important part of its history. It's surprising how many sellers are happy to part with their bike and accept your cash, but want to hang on to their photographs! In the latter event, you may be able to persuade the vendor to get a set of copies made.

12 What's it worth to you?
– let your head rule your heart!

Condition

If the bike you've been looking at is really ratty, then you've probably not bothered to use the marking system in chapter 9 – 30 minute evaluation. You may not have even got as far as using that chapter at all!

If you did use the marking system in chapter 9 you'll know whether the bike is in Excellent (maybe Concours), Good, Average or Poor condition or, perhaps, somewhere in between these categories.

To keep up to date with prices, buy the latest editions of the classic bike magazines and check the classified and dealer ads – these are particularly useful as they enable you to compare private and dealer prices. Most of the magazines run auction reports as well, which publish actual selling prices, as do the auction house websites. Most of the dealers will have up to date websites as well.

Values have been fairly stable for some time, but some models will always be more sought-after than others. For example, it's clear that an original CB750 K0 will command a high price, but if you want an all-round practical classic, then that's not the bike for you. Prices can go down as well as up, but the K0 and the various specialist frame kits (Seeley, Rickman etc) will remain the most sought-after.

Bear in mind that a bike that is truly a recent show winner could be worth more than the highest price usually seen. Assuming that the bike you have in mind is not in show/concours condition, then relate the level of condition that you judge it to be in with the appropriate price in the adverts. How does the figure compare with the asking price? Before you start haggling with the seller, consider what affect any variation from standard specification might have on the bike's value. This is a personal thing: for some, absolute originality is non-negotiable, while others see non-standard parts as an opportunity to pick up a bargain. Do your research in the reference books, so that you know the bike's spec when it left the factory. That way, you shouldn't end up paying a top-dollar price for a non-original bike.

If you are buying from a dealer, remember there will be a dealer's premium on the price.

Striking a deal

Negotiate on the basis of your condition assessment, mileage, and fault rectification cost. Also take into account the bike's specification. Be realistic about the value, but don't be completely intractable: a small compromise on the part of the vendor or buyer will often facilitate a deal at little real cost.

13 Do you really want to restore?

– it'll take longer and cost more than you think ...

Some people buy classic bikes because they love the restoration process: the strip down, the searching for rare parts and the careful rebuild. This page is not aimed at them. If you've never tackled a restoration before, it's a tempting prospect, to buy a cheap and tatty bike that 'just needs a few small jobs' to bring it up to scratch. But be honest with yourself – will you get as much pleasure from working on the bike as you will riding it? A good restoration takes time, and usually far longer than originally envisaged when those 'few small jobs' turn into big ones.

Even honest dirt can take some shifting.

Chrome can be replated.

The alternative is to hand the whole lot over to a professional, and the biggest cost involved there is not the new parts, but the sheer labour involved. From a financial point of view, this simply doesn't make sense with a Honda four. A professional restoration doesn't come cheap, and there are so many of these bikes around that the restoration cost will never be recouped by a high end value. If you still want to go the professional route, make it

A non-standard seat would need replacing.

absolutely clear what you want doing. Do you want the bike to be 100 per cent original at the end of the process, or simply useable? Do you want a concours finish, or are you prepared to put up with a few blemishes on the original parts?

Secondly, make sure that not only is a detailed estimate involved, but that it is more or less binding. There are too many stories of a person quoted one figure only to be presented with an invoice for a far larger one! Finally, check that the company you're dealing with has a good reputation – the owners club, or one of the reputable parts suppliers, should be able to make a few recommendations. Of course, if you can afford it but are short of time, a professional job could be just the thing.

Restoring the bike yourself requires a number of skills, which is fine if you already have them, but if you haven't it's not good to make your newly acquired bike part of the learning curve! Can you weld? Are you confident about building up an engine? Do you have a warm, well-lit garage with a solid workbench and good selection of tools?

Leaky forks can be fixed, but would you rather be riding?

Cracked panels can't be ignored.

Be prepared for a top-notch professional to put you on a lengthy waiting list or, if tackling a restoration yourself, expect things to go wrong and set aside extra time to complete the task. Restorations can stretch into years when things like life intrude, so it's good to have some sort of target date.

In fact, there's a lot to be said for a rolling restoration. This is not the way to achieve a concours finish, which can only really be achieved via a thorough nut-and-bolt rebuild, without the bike getting wet, gritty and salty in the meantime. And ultimately it will take longer. But riding helps keep your interest up as the bike's condition improves, and it's more affordable than trying to do everything in one go. And you'll get some fun out of the bike in the meantime.

Paint faults generally occur due to lack of protection/maintenance, or to poor preparation prior to a respray or touch-up. Some of the following conditions may be present in the bike you're looking at:

Orange peel

This appears as an uneven paint surface, similar to the appearance of the skin of an orange. The fault is caused by the failure of atomised paint droplets to flow into each other when they hit the surface. It's sometimes possible to rub out the effect with proprietary paint cutting/rubbing compound or very fine grades of abrasive paper. A respray may be necessary in severe cases. Consult a paint shop for advice.

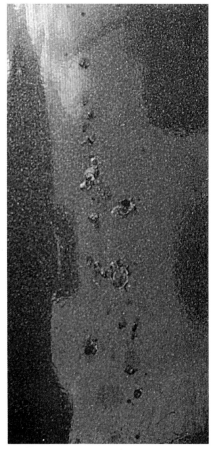

Cracking

Severe cases are likely to have been caused by too heavy an application of paint (or filler beneath the paint). Also, insufficient stirring of the paint before application can lead to the components being improperly mixed, and cracking can result. Incompatibility with the paint already on the panel can have a similar effect. To rectify it is necessary to rub down to a smooth, sound finish before respraying the problem area.

Crazing

Sometimes the paint takes on a crazed rather than a cracked appearance when the problems mentioned under 'cracking' are present. This problem can also be caused by a reaction between the underlying surface and the paint. Paint removal and respraying the problem area is usually the only solution.

Blistering

Almost always caused by corrosion of the metal beneath the paint. Usually perforation will be found in the metal and the damage will usually be worse than that suggested by the area of blistering. The metal will have to be repaired before repainting.

No way round it, rust means a respray.

A good spray job is a beautiful thing.

Micro blistering
Usually the result of an economy respray where inadequate heating has allowed moisture to settle on the vehicle before spraying. Consult a paint specialist, but damaged paint will have to be removed before partial or full respraying. Can also be caused by bike covers that don't 'breathe.'

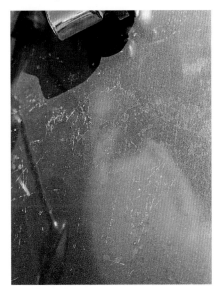

The paint's fine, but the top layer of clear lacquer is flaking off.

Fading
Some colours, especially reds, are prone to fading if subject to strong sunlight for long periods without the benefit of polish protection. Sometimes proprietary paint restorers and/or paint cutting/rubbing compunds will retrieve the situation. Often a respray is the only real solution.

Peeling
Often a problem with metallic paintwork when the sealing lacquer becomes damaged and begins to peel off. Poorly applied paint may also peel. The remedy is to strip and start again.

Dimples
Dimples in the paintwork are caused by the residue of polish (particularly silicone types) not being removed properly before respaying. Paint removal and repainting is the only solution.

15 Problems due to lack of use

– just like their owners, Honda fours need exercise!

Damp storage eventually leads to this sort of thing.

And once again, beware that Honda bugbear, the sticking brake caliper.

Tyres harden and crack if not used for long periods.

Like any piece of engineering, and indeed like human beings, Hondas deterioriate if they sit doing nothing for long periods. This is especially relevant if the bike is laid up for six months of the year, as some classic bikes are.

Rust

If the bike is put away wet, and/or stored in a cold, damp garage, the paint, metal and brightwork will suffer. Ensure the machine is completely dry and clean before going into storage, and if you can afford it, invest in a dehumidifier to keep the garage atmosphere dry.

Seized components

The brake caliper can seize on its pivot giving binding or non-working brakes. Cables are vulnerable to seizure too – the answer is to thoroughly lube them beforehand, and come into the garage to give them a couple of pulls once a week or so.

Tyres

If the bike's been left on its side stand, most of its weight is on the tyres, which will develop flat spots and cracks over time. Always leave the bike on its centre stand, which takes weight off the tyres.

Engine

Old, acidic oil can corrode bearings. Many riders change the oil in the spring, when they're putting the bike back on the road, but really it should be changed just before the bike is laid up, so that the bearings are sitting in fresh oil. While you're giving the cables their weekly exercise, turn the engine over slowly on the kickstart, ignition off. Don't start it though – running the engine for a short time does more harm than good, as it produces a lot of moisture internally, which the engine doesn't get hot enough to burn off. That will attack the engine internals and the silencers.

Battery/electrics

Either remove the battery and give it a top-up charge every couple of weeks, or connect it up to a battery top-up device such as the Optimate, which will keep it permanently fully charged. Damp conditions will allow fuses and earth connections to corrode, storing up electrical troubles for the spring. Eventually, wiring insulation will harden and fail.

Auctioneers

Bonhams
www.bonhams.com

British Car Auctions (BCA)
www.bca-europe.com or
www.british-car-auctions.co.uk

Cheffins
www.cheffins.co.uk

Dorset Vintage & Classic Auctions
www.dvca.co.uk

eBay
www.ebay.com

H&H
www.classic-auctions.co.uk

Shannons
www.shannons.com.au

Silver
www.silverauctions.com

Clubs across the world
Honda Owners Club GB
www.hoc.org.uk

**Vintage Japanese Motorcycle Club
(VJMC) UK**
www.vjmc.com

VJMC North America
www.vjmc.org

VJMC Australia
www.vjmc.org.au

VJMC New Zealand
Ross & Judy Charlton
– email: ross.judy@xtra.co.nz

Joining the club is a good move.

VJMC France
Denis O'Brien – 536 Rue Josepa
Vallot, Chamonix, France 74400.
(tel: 334 50535046)

VJMC Norway
Lars Chr Dahl – Solveien 112, 1162
Oslo 11, Norway. (tel: 00 47 2 229 6212)
– email: lcd@benly.no

VJMC Portugal/Algarve
Neil Beever (tel: 00 35 1 281 951117)

Honda Riders Club of America
www.hrca.honda.com

www.sohc4.net
Lots of information for all Honda sohc
fours

Specialists

We haven't attempted to list all the Honda specialists, but here's a selection from the UK. This list does not imply recommendation and is not deemed to be comprehensive.

Rising Sun Restorations
John Wyatt 01423 358004
www.risingsunrestoration.com

David Silver Spares (All Honda spares)
01728 833020
www.davidsilverspares.co.uk

Lings Honda (All Honda spares)
01379 853213
www.lings.com

On All Fours (400/4 spares)
0114 288 9465

Oxford Classic Honda (bikes and s/h spares)
01865 771166
www.classichondamotorcycles.co.uk

CMS (spares)
www.cmsnl.com

Books

Not all of these books are in print, but www.amazon.com may have secondhand copies. At autojumbles, look out for original handbooks and parts lists.

Honda CB350 and 400 Fours Performance Portfolio, RM Clarke, Brooklands Books

Honda CB500 and 550 Fours Performance Portfolio, RM Clarke, Brooklands Books,

Honda CB750 Gold Portfolio, RM Clarke, Brooklands Books,

Honda CB750 Super Profile, Pete Shoemark, Haynes Publishing, 1983

Original Honda CB750: Restorer's Guide, John Wyatt, Bay View Books, 2005

The Honda Story, Ian Falloon, Haynes Publishing, 2005

17 Vital statistics
– essential data at your fingertips

Listing the vital statistics of every Honda four variant would take far more room than we have here, so we've picked three representative models:

Max speed
1975 CB400F: 108mph
1976 CB550F: 105mph
1971 CB750: 121mph

Engine
1975 CB400F: SOHC four-cylinder, bore x stroke 51 x 50mm, 408cc, compression ratio 9.4:1, 37bhp @ 8500rpm
1976 CB550F: SOHC four-cylinder, bore x stroke 58.5 x 50.6mm, 544cc, compression ratio 9.0:1, 50bhp @ 8500rpm
1971 CB750: SOHC four-cylinder, bore x stroke 61 x 63mm, 736cc, compression ratio 9.0:1, 67bhp @ 8000rpm

Gearbox
1975 CB400F: 1st 2.733:1, 2nd 1.800:1, 3rd 1.375:1, 4th 1.111:1, 5th 0.965:1, 6th: 0.866:1
1976 CB550F: 1st 2.353:1, 2nd 1.636:1, 3rd 1.269:1, 4th 1.036:1, 5th 0.900:1
1971 CB750: 1st 2.500:1, 2nd 1.708:1, 3rd 1.333:1, 4th 1.097:1, 5th 0.939:1

Brakes
1975 CB400F: Front hydraulic disc, rear drum
1976 CB550F: Front hydraulic disc, rear drum
1971 CB750: Front hydraulic disc, rear drum

Electrics
1975 CB400F: 12-volt alternator
1976 CB550F: 12-volt alternator
1971 CB750: 12-volt alternator

Weight
1975 CB400F: 375lb
1976 CB550F: 450lb
1971 CB750: 522lb

Major change points by model years
1969
750: Original CB750, first 7400 or so with sandcast cases. Louvred side panels, all-cable throttles, small seat hump, plastic instrument lenses.

1971
500: CB500 K0 launched.
750: Updated K1 (launched US late '69). Single throttle cable drawing a beam, restyled airbox and new badges on oil tank, white tank lettering, black front brake caliper.

1972
350: CB350 launched.
500: Updated as CB500 K1, though no major changes.
750: K2 with restricted silencers, altered rear shocks and metal (not plastic) chainguard. Warning light panel between instruments.

1973
500: Updated as CB500 K2, with new instruments and colours.
750: K3 for US with improved forks and 5-way adjustable shocks, new tank graphics, restricted air intake, front disc water guard and running lights in indicators. K2 elsewhere has first two improvements.

1974

550: CB550 K0 launched.
750: K4 for USA/Japan, K2 elsewhere. Only 3 vertical braces in cylinder head side fins. K4 has ratio indicator on gearbox.

1975

400: CB400F replaces CB350. Red or blue, early bikes had matt black side panels.
550: CB550 K1 update (few changes) and new sportier CB550F1, latter with 4-into-1 exhaust and warning light panel between instruments.
750: K5 for USA, K2/4 elsewhere. K5 has bigger indicators and rubber-tipped flip-up sidestand and left-hand (not right-hand) petrol tap. Super Sport F1 with lower gearing, 4-into-1, rear disc, stronger swing arm, lower bars.

1976

400: Pillion pegs moved from swingarm to frame mounting.
750: K6 with stronger swingarm, detuned engine, no chain oiler. CB750A Hondamatic with semi-auto transmission launched (not sold in UK).

1977

400: Locking fuel filler cap.
550: CB550 F1 replaced by F2 with detail changes.
750: K7 with F1-type engine and single carburettor acceleration pump. Plainer silencers, 17-inch rear wheel and wider rear tyre, O-ring chain, flush fuel filler. F2 replaces F1 with bigger valve 70bhp engine, black finish, Comstar five-spoke wheels, FVQ shocks and new forks. 750A1 has 4-into-2 exhaust.

1978

400: CB400F2 replaces 400F, in maroon or yellow with pinstriping on tank. Filler cap moved to one side. Mechanically unchanged.
750: K8 for US with two-tier seat, minor

engine changes. 750A2 with Comstar wheels.

1979

400: CB400F2 dropped.
650: CB650 launched to fill gap between 550 and new dohc 750.

1980

650: CB650 Nighthawk factory custom launched, the final sohc Honda four.

Engine/frame numbers
CB350F
CB350F (1972-73)
    Frame from CB350F-1000001
    Engine from CB350E-1000001
CB350F (1974)
    Frame from CB350F-2000001
    Engine from CB350E-2000001

CB400F
CB400F (1975-77)
    Frame from 1007709-1073399
    Engine from 1007720-1069245
CB400 F2 (1978-79)
    Frame from 1074740-1085944
    Engine from 1069242-1086660

CB500/550
CB500 K0 (1971)
    Frame from CB500-1000001
    Engine from CB500E-1000001
CB500 K1 (1972)
    Frame from CB500-2000001
    Engine from CB500E-2000001
CB500 K2 (1973)
    Frame from CB500-2100001
    Engine from CB500E-2100001
CB550 K0 (1974)
    Frame from CB550-1000001
    Engine from CB550E-1000001
CB550 K1 (1975)
    Frame from CB550-1200005
    Engine from CB550E-1029182
CB550 K2 (1976)
    Frame from CB550-1230001
    Engine from CB550E-1067334

CB550 K3 (1977)
  Frame from CB550-2000007
  Engine from CB550E-2000001
CB550 K4 (1978)
  Frame from CB550-2100001
  Engine from CB550E-2100001
CB550 F1 (1975)
  Frame from CB550F-1000002
  Engine from CB550E-1100004
CB550 F1 (1976)
  Frame from CB550F-2000003
  Engine from CB550E-1109887
CB550 F1/F2 (1977)
  Frame from CB550-2100001
  Engine from CB550E-1135380

CB650
CB650 (1979)
  Frame from CB650-RC03-2002472
  Engine from CB650E-RC03E-2002513
CB650 (1980)
  Frame from CB650-RC05-2100002
  Engine from CB650E-RC05E-2100009
CB650 (1981)
  Frame from JH2RC0507BM00013
  Engine from RC03E-2200004
CB650 (1982)
  Frame from JH2RC0509CM300003
  Engine from RC03E-2300001
CB650 Nighthawk (1980)
  Frame from CB650SC RC05-210008
  Engine from CB650SC RC03E-210001
CB650 Nighthawk (1981)
  Frame from JH2RC0509CM300003
  Engine from RC03E-220004
CB650 Nighthawk (1982)
  Frame from JH2RC0808CM000013
  Engine from RC03E-2000018

CB750
CB750 (1969-70)
  Frame from 1000001
  Engine from E1000001

CB750 K1 (Aug 1970-Nov 1971)
  Frame from 1053399
  Engine from E1044806
CB750 K2 (Nov 1971-Sept 1972)
  Frame from 2000001
  Engine from E2000001
CB750 K3 (Sept 1972-June 1973)
  Frame from 2200001
  Engine from E2200001
CB750 K4 (June 1973-May 1974)
  Frame from 2300001
  Engine from E2300001
CB750 K5 (May-Dec 1974)
  Frame from 2500001
  Engine from E2372115
CB750 K6 (Dec 1974-June 1976)
  Frame from 2540001
  Engine from E2428762
CB750 K7 (June 1976-May 1977)
  Frame from 2700002
  Engine from E2700001
CB750 K8 (May 1977-May 1978)
  Frame from 2800001
  Engine from E3000001
CB750 F1 (March 1975-Nov 1976)
  Frame from 2000003
  Engine from E2515094
CB750 F2 (Nov 1976-May 1977)
  Frame from 2100011
  Engine from E2600004
CB750 F3 (May 1977-May 1978)
  Frame from 2200001
  Engine from E3100001
CB750A (Dec 1975-Sept 1976)
  Frame from 7000001
  Engine from E7000001
CB750A1 (Sept 1976-May 1977)
  Frame from 7100001
  Engine from E7100001
CB750A2 (May-Oct 1977)
  Frame from 7200001
  Engine from E7200001

The Essential Buyer's Guide™ series

£9.99*/$19.95*

*prices subject to change • p&p extra • for more details visit www.veloce.co.uk or email info@veloce.co.uk

Also from Veloce –

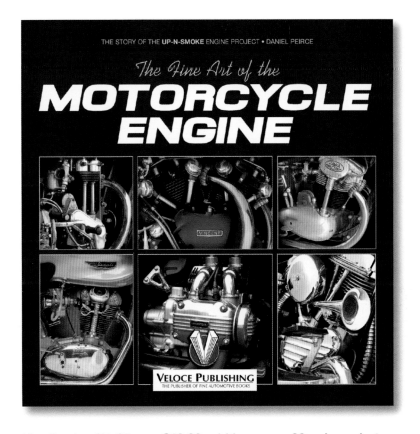

Hardback • 25x25cm • £19.99 • 144 pages • 89 colour photos
• ISBN: 978-1-845841-74-4

Professional photographer Dan Peirce presents 64 stunning pictures from his popular 'Up-n-Smoke' engine project. The book also tells the story behind the project and how it took years to bring it from an inspired idea to a tangible reality. "Pornography for Gearheads" – *Cycle World* magazine

Also from Veloce –

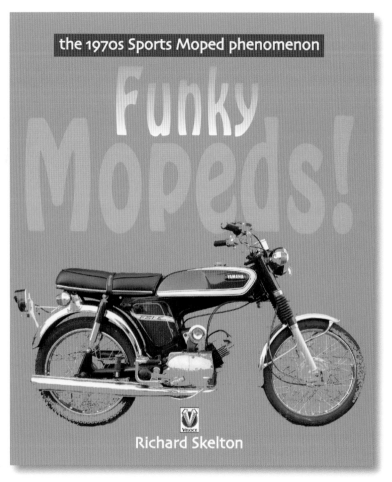

the 1970s Sports Moped phenomenon

Funky Mopeds!

Richard Skelton

Paperback • 25x20.7cm • £14.99 • 144 pages • 150+ colour photos • ISBN: 978-1-845840-78-5

A change in the legal definition of a 'Moped' (motorcycle with pedals) led to an explosion of high-performance 50cc machines which were every teenager's dream during the 1970s. Here's a colourful celebration of those fantastic machines and the culture of the 1970s.

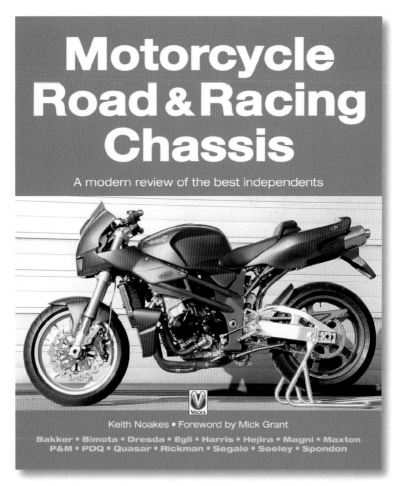

Index